Title: 3 Days of Fasting & Prayer

Copyright (c) 2012 Purpose Clinic Publishing:

Tel: +27110518220 / +27728406419

Email: publish@purposeclinic.com

Purpose Clinic books and materials maybe purchased for educational, business, or sales promotional use. Online editions are also available for most titles. For more information, contact our sales department: publish@purposeclinic.com

All rights reserved. Except as permitted under the South Africa Copyright Act 98 of 1978, no part of this publication may be reproduced, distributed, or transmitted in any form or by any means, or stored in a database or retrieval system, without the prior written permission of the publisher. The information in this book is distributed on an 'as is' basis, without warranty. Although every precaution has been taken in the preparation of this work, neither the authors nor Purpose Clinic Publishing shall have any liability to any person or entity with respect to any loss or damage caused or alleged to be caused directly or indirectly by the information contained in this work.

While every precaution has been taken in the preparation of this book, the publisher and author assume no

responsibility for errors, omissions, or for damages resulting from the use of the information contained herein.

ISBN: 978-1-920664-06-0

3 Days
of
Fasting
& Prayer

Apostle
Charles Magaiza

INTRODUCTION

My fasting journey began at an early age in life. The challenge from that time was always a guide to help one through the time of intense commitment in prayer. The need is always there to be able to hear the voice of God which is important at this time of your spiritual journey otherwise the time of fasting will go to waste. The Holy Spirit began to inspire me to put books together to help believers as they go through their journey of fasting and prayer. The fast should not be just the putting away of food but a time to seek and find the face of God. The Bible tells us,

> Ask, and it shall be given you; seek, and ye shall find; knock, and it shall be opened unto you: For every one that asketh receiveth; and he that seeketh findeth; and to him that knocketh it shall be opened.
>
> (Matthew 7:7-8 KJV)

Fasting registers in God's presence as deep desire expressed. It is asking, seeking and knocking. When one does this, the promise is sure as expressed in the word of God- you will receive, find and the door will be opened for you. As you begin these three days of prayer and fasting, I want to believe with you for answers. Whatever matter you are praying for must be settled. When you seek God's kingdom first, He will add all these other things to you. To desire is to covet for something deeply.

Many have asked me what the formula for fasting is. The question is, is there a formula? The Bible does not clearly spell out on the minute detail of fasting but from experience, there are some things that have become clearer to me.

My encounter with God

Years back in 1995, I had just finished high school waiting to go to university. At the beginning of that year, I felt it upon my heart to begin to seek The Lord as to what he desired for my life. You see, I didn't want to go through life in countless circles that had no meaning in them. It is easy to do that at this stage in life. I wanted to get things right early. I decided to begin a forty day fast. It was something I had not attempted before. Don't get scared, my forty days were surely different from the ones that Moses undertook. I normally say to people when you say days of fasting, it must be supper to supper but this is not a prescription. Others want to eat in the morning before beginning their fast at 6am. If you feel in your heart that it is correct, then put your faith even on your process and how you are doing it. When it's days and nights, then it means there is no eating at all until the fast comes to an end.

As I went along with my fast and prayer, it was imperative that I also took time to study the word and also listen to inspiring messages. You see, what you see and hear during this time is important. You do not want any interference at this time. In our busy world today, they are many things that can mute the voice of God for us. Your fast must therefore go beyond the abstinence from food. It must move to abstinence from all other distractions including those TV programs and even some of the things we read. This book intends to help you keep your focus during your three days and nights fast or just the days.

As I continued with my fast in 1995, the 21st day was noteworthy. It had seemed as if God was not saying anything during all the other days. This can seem to be the situation in your fast, don't despair. He is a speaking God and He will speak to you. Remember Daniel at the time he undertook his twenty one days of fasting and prayer. There seemed to be no answer until the very final day.

Then said he unto me, Fear not,

Daniel: for from the first day that thou didst set thine heart to understand, and to chasten thyself before thy God, thy words were heard, and I am come for thy words.

But the prince of the kingdom of Persia withstood me one and twenty days: but, lo, Michael, one of the chief princes, came to help me; and I remained there with the kings of Persia.

Now I am come to make thee understand what shall befall thy people in the latter days: for yet the vision is for many days.

(Daniel 10:12-14 KJV)

The angel announced to him that from the first day that he began his fast, his petition was heard in heaven and an angel was dispatched. The prince of the kingdom of Persia withstood the angel for twenty one days. By all means the devil was trying to prevent answers that were due to Daniel. You see, the prince of Persia here is a demonic stronghold that had spiritual dominance over Persia. It took the deployment of Michael, an angel of higher authority to come and help release the angel that was carrying Daniel's answer. This is why it is important to pray and fast as there are demonic strongholds already geared up to block everything answer or blessing that is due to you.

On the day when I finished my night prayers I went to bed at around 10pm. At around 11pm The Lord came into my room. My spirit was lifted from my body and I could see my body lying there on the bed. There was such an intense presence of God in the room. As my spirit was floating there just below the ceiling, I started to look around the room. I had a little poster that I had put on my wall that had written on it some things to do with success. Right on this paper, the words were written:

"**Others are busy seeking my will for their lives. What is my will for your life?**" It was clear and I stammered any answer, "**Soul winning Lord.**" When I said that, the Lord seemed pleased with it and my spirit descended back towards my body and the moment it touched my body, I immediately jolted out of bed. There was still an intense presence in the room when I physically woke up.

Nothing Is Impossible

There is no situation that prayer and fasting cannot change. There are issues that are only dealt with and changed by fasting and prayer. This is why understanding of this subject is critical. Jesus spoke and said,

> And Jesus said unto them, Because of your unbelief: for verily I say unto you, If ye have faith as a grain of mustard seed, ye shall say unto this mountain, Remove hence to yonder place; and it shall remove; and nothing shall be impossible unto you. Howbeit this kind goeth not out but by prayer and fasting. (Matthew 17:20-21 KJV)

The disciples were faced with a demon possessed child needing deliverance. Their attempt to cast out the demon was futile. When Jesus came, he rebuked the demon and it left. The disciples in private asked why they had failed to cast the demon out. The master pointed to their unbelief and also the fact that the type of demon they were facing needed prayer and fasting for it to be cast out. Yes, prayer and fasting has the ability of stirring your faith to a higher level.

Listen child of God, nothing shall be impossible in this season of prayer and fasting. You might have tried all else and it failed, believe today that your prayer and fasting will get answers.

And Jesus looking upon them saith, With men it is impossible, but not with God: for with God all things are possible. (Mark 10:27 KJV).

You can turnaround that doctor's report. You can turnaround that job situation. Yes, that situation of lack can be turned into abundance. Is it a child that has gone astray, this can be resolved as you pray and fast! Cancers must bow to the name of Jesus as you pray and fast. Childlessness must bow. You shall conceive and bear children. Your situation will come face to face with deity this time and every demon that was responsible for backing up the situation has to bow to the power that you are generating as you pray and fast.

I pray for you that as you begin this journey, may heaven be attentive to your prayers. As you call on Jehovah in the name of Jesus, may there be instant answers. May angels be put on standby to bring answers to you speedily!

I pray for you as you undertake this important journey; that God's Spirit will overshadow you as he did Mary and she conceived and bore a son. May you hear the voice of God in a loud and clear manner! May every desire that you have that has prompted you to begin this fast be met fully in the name of Jesus.

CHAPTER 1

Is this not the fast I have chosen?

I have many recollections and testimonies of how fasting and prayer brought about many victories in the past. Stubborn cases that I faced had to bow down to fasting and prayer. There are times I needed strength to do God's work, I prayed and the strength came. Every big decision needed the backing of prayer and fasting. The day to day demands of building an international ministry could overwhelm one but when time is taken to fast and pray, God gives direction.

There are basic instructions that are given in the word on the nature of fasting.

Is not this the fast that I have chosen? to loose the bands of wickedness,

to undo the heavy burdens, and to let the oppressed go free,

and that ye break every yoke? Is it not to deal thy bread to the hungry,

and that thou bring the poor that are cast out to thy house? when thou seest the naked, that thou cover him; and that thou hide not thyself from thine own flesh? Then shall thy light break forth as the morning, and thine health shall spring forth speedily: and thy righteousness shall go before thee; the glory of the Lord shall be thy rereward.

(Isaiah 58:6-8 KJV)

When we fast, it's not for us to be proud and prove to the world that we are very religious. It is not to build our own self righteousness. Isaiah 58 shows us the kind of fast that God is interested in. When you fast, it must result in the following:

- Breaking the chains of injustice

- Get rid of exploitation around you

- Freeing the oppressed

- Canceling of debts

Fasting has in its centre compassion, the love for mankind and desiring God to equip us to reach out to people and be instruments of His power. There is no room for selfishness and pride in your fast. God wants to see you:

- Share your food with the hungry
- Invite the homeless poor into your homes
- Clothing the ill
- Being available for your own families

Your fast must transform you! It is a wakeup call that causes you to take an audit of your own life and evaluate your own attitudes towards God and man. When you do this, there are many promises in the word of God for the one who fasts. Below are some of these promises:

- The lights will turn on for you; your life will turn around at once

- Your righteousness will pave your way

- The Lord will protect you and make your path clear

- When you pray, God will answer

- God will direct you

- Your light will shine in the darkness

- You will receive a full life even in difficult circumstances

- The works of your hands will be blessed.

- You will be a well watered garden, a spring with a constant supply of water

- You will be a rain maker in your life, a light people run to for answers.

"Fasting and prayer are proper means for the bringing down of Satan's power against us, and the fetching in of divine power to our assistance. Fasting is of use to put an edge upon prayer; it is an evidence and instance of humiliation which is necessary in prayer, and is a means of mortifying some corrupt habits, and of disposing the body to serve the soul in prayer. When the devil's interest in the soul is confirmed by the temper and constitution of the body, fasting must be joined with prayer, to keep under the body."

(Matthew Henry Commentary).

Fasting will free your mind to hold effective communication with God. It stirs the power within and sets your faith on new dimensions. It is a discipline that every believer must learn to engage in for the advancement of God's kingdom and for their personal progress.

CHAPTER 2

Morning- Day 1

My sheep hear my voice,

and I know them, and they follow me: And I give unto them eternal life; and they shall never perish, neither shall any man pluck them out of my hand.

(John 10:27-28 KJV)

Today, the focus is to hear the voice of God. He is always speaking; the question has always been whether our ears are attune to hearing him speak. Sheep are amazing creatures; they are gentle but always require a shepherd to lead them. Otherwise they will wonder off in all directions. The Psalmist understood this and declares the Lord is my shepherd.

The LORD is my shepherd; I shall not want.

He maketh me to lie down in green pastures: he leadeth me beside the still waters.

He restoreth my soul: he leadeth me in the paths of righteousness for his name's sake.

Yea, though I walk through the valley of the shadow of death, I will fear no evil: for thou art with me; thy rod and thy staff

they comfort me. Thou preparest a table before me in the presence of mine enemies: thou anointest my head with oil; my cup runneth over. Surely goodness and mercy shall follow me all the days of my life: and I will dwell in the house of the LORD for ever.

(Psalm 23:1-6 KJV)

The point in this fast is the issue of leadership. You must relinquish that to the Lord so that he can give you perfect guidance on where you should go, what you should do and how you should do it. Your lifetime must not be wasted going around in endless circles. This morning therefore your prayer must be focused in giving God full room to operate in your life. To be the leader and shepherd! The benefits of this are clear in the scripture- He will break the endless circles and cause you to lie down in green pasture and lead you besides still waters. Your soul will be restored and will lead you into paths of righteousness. The world today has too many things that can contaminate your soul. As He leads and you follow, you will receive restoration in your soul.

Kenneth E. Hagin in his book How You can Be Led by the Spirit of God says, "Many times we seek guidance by means other than the way God said. When we do, we get into trouble. We sometimes judge how God is leading by what our physical senses tell us."

Your spirit man must gain the ascendancy over your flesh. You are a spirit being and the Holy Spirit speaks directly to your spirit.

I pray for you this morning that there be a complete cleansing of your soul. That you be restored to a place of fellowship with God. I pray that the voice of the Lord would become clearer to you in Jesus' name.

Declare this,

Thank you Father for this day of fasting as I desire deeply to hear your voice! Thank you for your protection, leadership and guidance at this special time. I ask that you bless my time of fasting and prayer today so that it is meaningful and comes with great results. I thank you in Jesus' name. Amen

Evening- Day 1

Then I proclaimed a fast there, at the river of Ahava, that we might afflict ourselves before our God, to seek of him a right way for us, and for our little ones, and for all our substance. For I was ashamed to require of the king a band of soldiers and horsemen to help us against the enemy in the way: because we had spoken unto the king, saying, The hand of our God is upon all them for good that seek him; but his power and his wrath is against all them that forsake him. So we fasted and besought our God for this: and he was intreated of us.

(Ezra 8:21-23 KJV)

Our God is the leader and must be given the room to lead us. The above scripture shows us the story of Ezra, how he had to proclaim a corporate fast because of the great task that was ahead of them. There was need for hearing the voice of God on the right way. This fast involved even their children. It is good to let our children also participate in seasons of prayer and fasting. They will grasp this important tool which they can make use of in their future life.

They put their faith in God as they did not want to rely on man. Thank God he heard them and helped them through the critical time. Man can be unpredictable, it is better to put your trust in God.

> With him is an arm of flesh; but with us is the LORD our God to help us, and to fight our battles. And the people rested themselves upon the words of Hezekiah king of Judah.
>
> (2Ch 32:8 KJV)

Cursed is he that leans on the help of man. Your prayer today is to entreat the hand of God to help in every battle you have been facing in life. It doesn't matter what the situation is. It might look severe and hard to manage. I want you to know today that with God you can sail through this situation. Is it a disease or a financial crisis? Is it an addiction or a child that has gone astray? Our God will bring help at this time as you pray. Yes, he can correct every situation as he is an all powerful God.

I pray for you tonight that God's hand will be visible on your life. That every situation that was stubborn bows to the name of Jesus! I address every demonic force or influence that was wrecking havoc in your life as we have been given power and authority to deal with these. You are rising in power and dominance over that situation in Jesus' name.

Declare this,

Father I thank you tonight for your faithfulness. Thank you for giving me the grace to lean on your word and on you for strength. Thank you for breathing life into my situation and offering me personal progress in the name of Jesus.

CHAPTER 3

Morning- Day 2

Until the spirit be poured upon us from on high, and the wilderness be a fruitful field, and the fruitful field be counted for a forest.

(Isa 32:15 KJV)

The Spirit of the Lord is the agent of the God head operating in our lives. He is alive and active in your life today. The outside circumstances might look chaotic; things might be out of place and out of joint. The Holy Spirit has the capacity to transform things for you today. His Spirit is present right now where you are. It is the same Holy Spirit that came on the day of Pentecost and turned the disciples that were discouraged and fearful into courageous people. They were able to leave the room they were in and instantly began to minister to other people (Acts 2:14-17 KJV).

But Peter, standing up with the eleven, lifted up his voice, and said unto them, Ye men of Judaea, and all *ye* that dwell at Jerusalem, be this known unto you, and hearken to my words:

For these are not drunken, as ye suppose, seeing it is *but* the third hour of the day.

But this is that which was spoken by the prophet Joel;

And it shall come to pass in the last days, saith God, I will pour out of my Spirit upon all flesh: and your sons and your daughters shall prophesy, and your young men shall see visions, and your old men shall dream dreams:

You too must be enthused with this power this morning. It is this power that turns wildernesses into fruitful fields. It does not matter what was dying and was unfruitful around you, allow the Holy Spirit to take over and he will turn things around for your good today. The Holy Spirit is creating the right atmosphere in your life. Fear not those that were saying there is no way for you; God is the way this morning. He makes a way where there seems to be no way. He is the way the truth and the life (John 14:6).

I pray for you this morning that the Spirit of the Lord invades every cell in your body. As you fast, may difficult situations be turned around! You will see the hand of God in every area of your life today.

Declare this,

The Spirit of The Lord has been poured out. I get ready for supernatural ability, enablement, power and conquest today. I challenge the unchallenged. I go for exploits in Jesus' name.

Evening- Day 2

For the seed shall be prosperous; the vine shall give her fruit, and the ground shall give her increase, and the heavens shall give their dew; and I will cause the remnant of this people to possess all these things.(Zec 8:12 KJV)

The circle of life consists of seed time and harvest. Every day of our lives we are seeding and harvesting. We seed words, money, love, compassion, favour and many other things. Today, I want to believe with you that all good seed that you have sown will be prosperous and you will reap a good harvest. It is the grace of the Lord that causes any work that you do to yield fruit. There are some that are toiling day and night and nothing comes from it. They are tilling the ground and they harvest nothing. Tonight, believe God for this grace that can lift you from nothing to something. This grace that can change your environment!

You will possess all things by the grace of God at work in you tonight.

> But upon mount Zion shall be deliverance, and there shall be holiness; and the house of Jacob shall possess their possessions.
>
> (Oba 1:17 KJV)

It is time to possess your possessions. There are things that are due to you that the enemy has been stealing from you. This fast is a journey to the peak of mount Zion, the dwelling place of our God. As you have committed yourself to this fast- there must be recovery of the lost and the stolen. Burdens must be lifted up tonight. Discard all fear, confront every situation that was standing against you and demand back what is yours. There will be restoration in your life during this fast.

I pray for you tonight that there be a recovery of everything that you have lost. May angels be deployed on your behalf to recover stolen goods, time, relationships and everything else! You will possess your possessions.

Declare this,

I decree and declare my SEASON for ADVANCEMENT has come. I announce in every CORNER in the SPIRIT realm that it is my TURN to PROGRESS. Every demon that kept me back is embarrassed in Jesus' name.

CHAPTER 4

Morning- Day 3

Go, gather together all the Jews that are present in Shushan, and fast ye for me, and neither eat nor drink three days, night or day: I also and my maidens will fast likewise; and so will I go in unto the king, which *is* not according to the law: and if I perish, I perish.

(Esther 4:16 KJV)

Congratulations you are in your final day of this fast. When you engage in a time of fasting, it is a sacrifice. This morning, we look at the story of Esther. There are many lessons in this story. She comes from a position where she had nothing to being the queen of a vast kingdom. She was just an orphan girl. Her circumstances did not prepare her for what she became. God surely takes people from nothing to something.

The Jews at this time where faced with a crisis that would wipe them off the face of the earth. There conspiracy against them was severe they would be attacked across the whole kingdom. There was a need for them to act drastically and prevent the impending danger. They declared a fast for the Jews. For three days and nights they would fast and not eat anything. They were asking God for favour. You see there was a protocol set in the kingdom on how and when to appear before the king. There was need for favour to break the common protocol. Queen Esther shows her commitment to this and she was ready to appear before the king after the fast. Her faith was ignited after the fast and she did not care if she perished.

As you progress with this fast, your faith must sky rocket, it should allow you to break protocol. You must challenge the unchallenged. Closed doors will open, prison doors will be broken. It is your season to flourish. Let your faith triumph, let it be ignited for the next level.

I pray for you today, that the grace of God that lifts one up causes you to excel in all areas. That grace that turns failure to success, fear to faith, pain to strength, poverty to prosperity, and opposition to opportunity.

Declare this,

I declare increase and a bursting forth of favor in my life. I speak speed and fruitfulness over every area of my life this morning. It's time for the world to know that I carry the blessing.

Evening- Day 3

And ought not this woman, being a daughter of Abraham, whom Satan hath bound, lo, these eighteen years, be loosed from this bond on the sabbath day? (Luke 13:16 KJV)

Who you are related to and whose child you are matters. Because of this, you ought to know that as a child of Abraham, there are benefits that accrue to you. There will be opposition to your accessing these benefits but remain resolute in your faith.

For eighteen years, this woman could not stand. She was bent double and suffered from this infirmity. When Jesus saw her, he was moved with compassion and spoke to her, "Woman thou art loosed from your infirmity." When he laid hands on her she was made whole.

Healing is bread for the children of Abraham. Wealth is a benefit for the sons and daughters of Abraham. Being born again qualifies you for these blessings. Today, arise against every contenting word trying to oppose your access to your benefits. Psalms 103:2 records, "Bless the Lord, O my soul, and forget not all his benefits."

As you conclude this fast, lay hold on your benefits! Develop stubborn faith that does not relinquish anything to the devil. There are a lot of things that have been shaken during this fast, continue declaring the word of God even circumstances are looking negative.

I pray for you today, that you awaken to the blessings and benefits that accrue to you. That your ears be deaf to every voice that wants to stop your access to these benefits! I rebuke every spirit of infirmity that kept you limited.

Declare this,

I am a son of Abraham. I am loosed from any infirmity the devil was afflicting me with. I speak freedom from the crown of my head to my toes.

CONCLUSION

Congratulations on the conclusion of your fast. God has surely heard you and your petitions have been recorded in heaven. This is the time to rejoice and thank God for coming through on your requests.

Remember, your God loves you and He keeps watching over His word to perform it in your life. Don't despair; believe Him that he has already answered.

Now faith is the substance of things hoped for, the evidence of things not seen.

(Heb 11:1 KJV)

Your faith must speak for you today. I see you winning, I see you rejoicing. The victory shout is in your camp today.

DECLARATIONS & PRAYER POINTS

1. Today, deep seated lingering disorders must disappear. May the LIFE of God bring healing to your body, soul and spirit! You will FLOURISH in this season. Say I RECEIVE!

2. Today I declare protection from above over you, your family and loved ones. I BANISH tragedies and accidents. His angels have taken charge over you. Say I AGREE!

3. Today I declare deliverance from bad habits. I COMMAND every demon responsible for fueling that habit to LOOSE you in Jesus' name. Say I RECEIVE!

4. Today I speak to every fear and phobia that the enemy has used to limit, plunder, destroy and rob you of progress. Every word or symbol he has used to inspire fear is destroyed. Freedom is yours! Say AMEN!

5. Today your NAME is being remembered where it matters. Your FILE is being brought from the bottom drawer. They will look for your CV in the deleted items. Your set time has come in JESUS' name. Say I RECEIVE!

6. Today, there is a RESHUFFLE. Angels are on deployment to change THINGS in your life. You are moving from the tail to the HEAD, from beneath to ABOVE and from failure to SUCCESS. Say AMEN!

7. I pray for you today for RESILIENCE in the midst of the storm. Take a new GRIP with your tired hands. This too will come to pass. I see a victory dance ahead. Say AMEN!

8. As I thought of you I heard the words 'DUE DATE.' You are DUE for promotion, DUE for healing; you are DUE for prosperity & DUE for success. You are DUE for that marriage! In this season, the celebrations are in your house. The party is yours and the speeches are in honour of you. You waited, now you will see your recompense! Shout "I AM DUE!"

9. Input determines output! For any positive action there is a positive result coming. For any negative action, be on the lookout for the revenge. Today, calibrate your measurements to the greatest intellect ever, the mind of Christ. Say THESE ARE MY MEASUREMENTS!

10. All the hills shall melt: I publicize it that the hill of disease is melting in your life. The hill of war and death is melting. Those social, economic and political hills are bowing down to the WORD. This is all by the Spirit of the LORD. Your lips shall again sing praises, you will yet taste sweet wine and you will partake of the best things in life. Your story is changing! Say I RECEIVE!

11. What swallowed Jonah ended up transporting him to dry ground because God had spoken! I heard the voice of God speaking to your limitation today. That which was stopping you must vomit you on dry ground. Agree with me as I declare a new beginning on dry ground in every area of your life. I say to that limitation, "TRANSPORT THAT HOLY CARGO TO DRY GROUND!" Shout THAT'S ME!

12. You are OVERCOMING because of the blood of Jesus. Solutions are coming to your business, marriage, family, job and everything that concerns you. The grip of the enemy is broken. Say AMEN,

13. You will possess your possessions. Anything that has been stolen, taken by force, plundered or siphoned from you with or without your knowledge must be RETURNED today. Shout AMEN!

14. I said TURNAROUND, TURNAROUND! I speak to every stubborn situation to release you today. It's your turn to do a victory dance. Say I RECEIVE!

15. As you sleep tonight, may the SPIRIT of The Lord HEAL and REPAIR your body. May renewal come into every bone, muscle, vein and organ in Jesus' name! Say AMEN!

16. I pray that life changing secrets be revealed to you today. Revolutions are beginning in your life as you become privy to hidden truths. Get ready and say I RECEIVE!

17. I declare the challenges around will not engulf you. Jesus stands with you as you stand with Him. You will be a witness of a great deliverance today. Say AMEN!

18. I prophesy the FALLING of every Babylon responsible for your sickness, lack of progress, joblessness and fear. You are coming out strong. Say AMEN!

19. As you sleep tonight, ANGELS are on deployment to deal with every demonic force that was working against you. You will wake up to great victories! Say I RECEIVE!

20. I prophesy those who spoiled shall be spoiled today. There is a sevenfold recovery of everything the enemy stole coming to you NOW. Say I RECEIVE!

21. As you sleep tonight, I heard the Spirit of God whisper the words 'Stubborn Mountains that stood against you are meeting their demise.' Get ready for a move of God. Say COUNT ME IN!

22. I declare the opening of closed doors. Doors of employment, finance, marriage, promotion and health are opening right NOW in Jesus' name. Say I RECEIVE!

23. As you sleep tonight, I heard the Holy Spirit whisper the word PURPOSE. May you wake up to an awareness of your assignment here on earth! I pray that your eyes be opened to see it. Say I AM READY!

24. I command every gate that the enemy was using to access your life closed NOW. Every marauding devil causing instability in your life is locked out today. Say I AGREE!

25. Today I speak to all forms of barrenness and declare that you will conceive and bear fruit. Every system must align despite opposing variables in Jesus' name. Say I RECEIVE!

26. As you sleep tonight may every word God has spoken in your life be fulfilled! The world will testify to the faithfulness of God as they look at your life. Say AMEN,

27. Today I speak increase in all areas of your life. May you increase in wisdom and stature! May you increase in favor with GOD and with man! Say AMEN!

28. There is a dividing of spoils today. Angels are come upon the enemy and they are taking back everything he had stolen from you. They are breaking all his armor which he trusted in. Receive your job back, receive your marriage, receive your children, and receive your wealth and health. Shout I RECEIVE!

29. Thus says The Lord, not by might nor by power but by my Spirit. Get ready for renewal, perfection, healing, favor and grace for the Spirit has taken over. Say AMEN!

30. Today I speak to sons and daughters of Abraham. I say be loosed from any infirmity the devil was afflicting you with. I speak freedom from the crown of your head to your toes. Say I RECEIVE!

RELATED TITLES

Made in the USA
Columbia, SC
28 June 2025

60025798R10039